Introduction

No matter where you are on Earth, insects and spiders were there first and in huge numbers! They are the most successful of all land animals, and among the most fascinating. Their life cycle and their ability to find food and defend themselves have guaranteed that they will outlast humans on this planet. For many of us, an insect or spider is something to be swotted, avoided or squealed at, but without them our lives and our environment would suffer enormously.

Contents

Read on to discover the giant world of small creatures...

Introducing insects

Insects are the most **numerous** and widespread of all animal groups, and there are many more **species** to be discovered. An insect has a hard external skeleton, an **exoskeleton**, divided into three **segments** (head, thorax and abdomen), six legs and a 3–4-stage lifecycle. They are found on **every** continent on Earth and in all **habitats**. Their ability to thrive is down to their senses, **adaptation** to different environments and their ability to communicate, organise and **breed** successfully. Being small has certainly helped insects to become so **dominant**.

Nine out of ten insect species eat plant food, such as sap, nectar or berries.

Ants use strength and teamwork to loosen a wild strawberry for the colony's larder

Extreme tolerance

The desert ant can briefly tolerate searing temperatures of 70°Celsius, and the aquatic dance fly larva does not freeze solid at temperatures of –22°Celsius.

Good to be small

Small works for insects: oxygen is used efficiently, there's less chance of being eaten and fewer moults required.

Did you know?

Insects first appeared on Earth 479 million years ago at the same time as the first land plants. This fossil is 150 million years old, but it is unmistakably a type of dragonfly.

A praying mantis grips a grasshopper in its spined front legs

Hunt for prey

Many insects are hunters with mouthparts that are large in comparison to body size. The praying mantis chases its prey and then strikes out with its sharp spined front legs. The antlion larva digs a pit, hides at the bottom with only its fangs exposed and waits for an ant to slip into the pit.

Hunt for a host

Many insects are parasites, which means they live in or on another animal (the host) and feed off its body or blood. Sometimes the host survives, sometimes not. Bedbugs and lice are parasites with a preference for human blood. Lice without the body heat generated by a host die within a week.

Head lice lay their eggs at the base of hairs

Noisy insect

Insect songs and calls attract mates. The cicada call can be heard a kilometre away.

Air holes

Insects do not breathe through their mouth. Instead air enters through openings, called spiracles, on the sides of their abdomen.

Flee or freeze

Insects migrate to avoid unsuitable climates and to find food – and some go to great lengths. Dragonflies cover 14,000 km on their India–South Africa return migration. Monarch butterflies in the US have a 7,700-km round trip, but many do not make it so females lay their eggs during the return journey.

Migrating monarch butterflies feeding on nectar

Insect life cycle

Insects have remarkable **reproductive** abilities, which have led to the vast number of insects in **nature**. Some estimate that for every human there are **200 million** insects. After depositing the **eggs**, many adult insects abandon their offspring. The eggs hatch into **larvae** or nymphs that eat, grow and moult – shed their exoskeleton – until they become **adults** ready to mate. In some insects a pupal stage follows the final moult. A **pupa** is a hard case that surrounds an insect like a caterpillar. A **caterpillar** goes into the pupa, metamorphosis occurs and a **butterfly** emerges.

Facts and figures

African driver ant
This social insect can lay 3–4 million eggs every 25 days.

Australian ghost moth
This nonsocial insect has a clutch of over 29,000 eggs with a further 15,000 eggs ready to lay.

Mayfly
A mayfly lives for 30 minutes to 24 hours. Its lifecycle is hatch, reproduce and die in quick succession.

Houseflies
A pair of houseflies could produce 190 quintillion (190 followed by 18 zeros) offspring in a five month season.

Termite queen
A queen termite is typically the oldest termite in the colony and she will live for around 15 years. The queen can lay about 30,000 eggs every day, which means she can produce 165 million eggs in her lifetime!

Winter moulting

Dragonfly nymphs pass the winter in water under sheets of ice and emerge as adults in spring. During this time, dragonflies can shed their exoskeleton 10 times.

Winter survival

Insect larvae that are buried in leaf litter or underground can survive winter temperatures. Survival of overwintered eggs is less likely.

Did you know?

A queen weaver ant protects and feeds her first egg clutch, but worker ants will mostly care for the following clutches. Only social insects, like ants and bees, care for their young.

A caterpillar went into the chrysalis (pupa), and now a common windmill butterfly emerges

A caterpillar stays in its chrysalis for 7-14 days.

A cicada frees itself through a split in the exoskeleton

Moult to grow

An insect sheds (moults) its hard exoskeleton in order to grow. Prior to moulting, a larva takes in extra air or water, then stops breathing for up to an hour while the exoskeleton splits and frees the animal. Some insects eat the old skin. During moulting, missing limbs are replaced and the larva is at its most vulnerable.

Mating gift

Some male insects give their female a gift before mating. The offering is usually food, like a dead insect, or a nutritious bodily secretion, but some males allow the female to eat a part of their body. The gift increases the chance of successful mating.

Number of moults

The firebrat, a small insect similar to a silverfish, moults 60 times. But a species of mealybug moults only twice during its life.

Caring earwigs

Earwigs lay only a small number of eggs, they lick them to keep the eggs infection-free.

A pair of robber (assassin) flies mating

Living incubators

Parasitoid wasps lay their eggs inside or on the body of other insects. As the larvae grow they feed on the host's tissues. When the larvae mature to pupate, they devour the host. One type of wasp picks ladybirds as hosts for its larvae because the ladybirds deter predators from the wasp's nest.

Larvae exit a hornworm, then build pupae on its body

Air and water insects

Insects were the **first** animals to fly. Almost all insects have wings, but not all wings will sustain **flight**. Flight means that insects can **colonise** almost anywhere to avoid danger and natural disasters and to find food. Insect wings inspired **aircraft** wings – curved on top and flat underneath. Only three per cent of **insects** live part or all of their life in water. Mosquito **larvae** dangle upside down **underwater** while caddisfly larvae anchor themselves to the bottom. Saucer bugs and water boatmen are **permanent** water dwellers that are well adapted to their **aquatic** habitat.

Facts and figures

Beating wings
A species of biting midge can beat its wings 1,046 times per second.

High jump
The high jump record of 71 cm goes to the spittlebug nymph.

Deepest
A non-biting midge larva found in the world's deepest lake, Lake Baikal in Russia, survives at depths of 1,360 metres.

Fastest runner
The fastest running insect is the Australian tiger beetle. It can cover 2.5 metres per second.

Flying speed
The male horsefly is the fasted flying insect in the world. It can reach speeds of 145 km per hour.

Ocean dwellers
Only five species of insects – sea skaters or halobates – can survive in open oceans.

Did you know?

The housefly beats its wings in a figure-of-eight shape 200–300 times a second. While its normal range is two kilometres, a housefly has been recorded flying 32 km on one journey.

After intercepting a fly in mid-flight, a dragonfly eats its kill on a leaf

Dragonflies are **Odonata species**, meaning 'toothed ones'.

Amazing eyesight

A dragonfly's eyes have 30,000 lenses that each captures an image. The images are merged into one picture in the brain. A dragonfly's eyes can see 360 degrees.

Serrated jaws

A dragonfly uses its strong, wide, serrated jaws to pulp its prey, first immobolising it by stripping off the prey's wings.

Taking to the air

Flying insects use flight to locate and catch food, to escape predators and other dangers and to find a mate. Insect wings go up and down, and forwards and backwards. They also rotate so that the trailing or leading edge changes angle (pitch). These help insects get lift, reduce drag and make rapid changes of direction.

Walking on water

Pond skaters can stand and move on water. Their long legs spread the weight of their light body. They use the middle pair of legs to row and the rear legs to steer, all without breaking the water's surface. A waxy coating makes pond skaters water-repellent.

The large sweep of a cabbage white butterfly's wings

Pond skater travels at one metre per second on water

Breathing underwater

Some mature aquatic insects use tubes that work like snorkels. The tube breaks the water surface to get air or it taps the air stored by some aquatic plants. Others, like great diving beetles, trap air among hairs on their body or under their wings. The air bubble can also 'collect' oxygen from the water to extend the time underwater.

A great diving beetle with air trapped under its wings

Factfile

Insect wings

Wings develop from the exoskeleton of an adult insect, and in some species only males have wings. Worker ants have usually lost their wings.

Damselfly

A damselfly can be identified by its wings, which lie against its body when at rest. All four wings are the same shape.

Thrip (thunderbug)

The thrip is unique in having two pairs of fringed wings. The fringes make its wings larger, making them capable of flight.

Ladybird

To fly, a ladybird raises its hard, colourful front wings, to allow the efficient rear wings to unfold and to do all the flying.

On land and below ground

All adult insects have six **legs**, which means that they can walk, scuttle, run and jump in their above ground **habitats** to find a mate, make a nest, evade a **predator** and obtain food. Some insects, like burrowing **beetles**, spend most of their lives in tunnels, **nests** and burrows, but others are underground only when larvae. The larvae of **grasshoppers**, like all insect larvae, are legless, so after hatching from **eggs** they wriggle to the surface as nymphs. They then grow legs that will let them leap, **claws** to cling to trunks with and **wings** that allow them to fly distances.

Facts and figures

High jump
The tiny springtail can jump 15 cm into the air. A human comparison would be jumping over the Eiffel Tower. Equally amazing is that it takes this insect only 18 milliseconds to ready its body to jump.

Weightlifting
The male rhinoceros beetle can lift 850 times its own weight. A human comparison would be lifting eight double-decker buses.

Pulling power
The horned dung beetle can pull 1,141 times its own weight. To equal this, a human would have to pull six packed double decker buses.

Vision
A bee can process what it sees five times faster than a human.

Super sense
When a female sawfly sent out a chemical message, 11,000 male sawflies responded.

Grasshoppers jump to escape enemies and can cover a metre in one leap.

A blue-winged grasshopper catapults itself into the air and then somersaults before landing

How they walk

When walking slowly an insect's legs move in a ripple-like wave down each side of the body, propelling the insect forwards.

... and run quickly

To 'run', an insect moves one leg on one side and two legs on the other side forwards then backwards; the other legs move backwards then forwards.

Did you know?

A periodical cicada lives underground for 17 years before emerging to moult and become an adult. Four weeks later it dies. This cicada is about to become an adult ready to mate.

A flea doing a mid-jump somersault

Jumping fleas

A 2–3-mm flea can jump 30 cm – a hundred times its length. It will travel through the air at speeds of up to 6.9 km per hour – onto an animal so that it can suck its blood. It jumps so high by pressing its toes into the ground while unleashing energy stored in pads above its multi-jointed hind legs.

It clicks!

The click beetle is named for the sound it makes when it jumps. It bends its head and thorax towards its abdomen and links them together with a spine. Unhooking the spine releases energy to make the 'click' and hurls the beetle into the air. It can do six somersaults during a jump. If it lands upside down, it rights itself in the same way.

Defying gravity

Insects can scale vertical surfaces and walk upside down because their feet end in tiny claws that hook into microscopically small 'toeholds' in surfaces. Some insects also have tiny hairs between the claws that secrete an oil that acts like an adhesive.

A click beetle ready to jump up to 30 cm into the air

Strong hook-like claws let this beetle dangle upside down from a leaf

Working together

Some insects live in communities that are highly **organised** and where each insect does a **job** that contributes to the community's survival. **Termites** and ants and some bee and wasp species are social insects that form **colonies**, usually in a nest. Workers produce and gather the materials to build the **nest**, find food, feed and care for the **queen** and her eggs and keep the nest disease-free. **Soldiers** defend the colony from predators and will fight to the death to save the colony. Forming colonies has made **social** insects the most numerous and **successful** of all animals.

Termite queen

When a termite queen-to-be leaves the mound for the last time, she scratches off her wings. She crawls back to the mound with a 'king' to mate, never to see daylight again.

30,000 eggs

Because she carries 30,000 eggs each day, a termite queen can be 10 cm in length, making her 100 times larger than a worker termite.

The **shafts** and **tunnels** in a **termite mound** ventilate the **nest** below.

Termite mounds in Australia and Africa can stand six metres tall, but the nest is actually underground

Did you know?

Ants touch each other with their antennae to detect pheromones. These chemicals let ants know if they are nest mates (if not, they may fight) and the direction of food or the nest.

Paper wasps repairing the colony's nest

Social wasps

The nests of social wasps, like yellow jackets and hornets, are made with chewed wood fibres mixed with wasp saliva. Some nests are built in trees, in holes in the ground or in buildings. Social wasp nests are for rearing the brood, not for storing food. Dead insects would rot too quickly.

Leaf-cutter ants

Processions of worker ants harvest leaves, chomping them down to a smaller size with a V-shaped blade in their jaw, then carry them to the nest. The leaves create a fungus that feeds the colony. Waste transporter ants keep the nest clean, even dumping dead ants on the waste heap.

Worker leaf-cutter ants dwarfed by a soldier ant

Courtier ants

This group of worker ants care, clean and feed the queen and the 'king' in the colony.

Jobs for all

A colony consists of one or more egg-laying queens and infertile female worker and solider ants. Male ants mate with a queen, then die.

Living larders

Most insects, like bees, that store food do so in their nest, but selected honeypot ants (the 'repletes') store a sugary nectar in their abdomens that swell to the size of cherries. Worker ants force-feed the repletes, then when food is scarce, the colony eats the nectar that the repletes throw up.

A honeypot ant regurgitating food for a worker ant

13

Busy bugs

Insects form essential links in **ecological** chains as plant-eaters, **predators** and parasites. Without insects, our planet would look very different. There would be no **pollination**, the land would be covered in dead organic matter and **waste** and some animal species would **starve**. Insects that feed on dead animals, excrement and decaying plants recycle **nutrients** back into the soil so that new plants can **grow**. Insect-eating animals, like sloths and **birds**, would die without insects to eat. But if there were no humans, only the human **louse** would be affected.

Facts and figures

What if there were no insects?

Lack of pollination
No pollination of plants would cause crops and pastures to fail, creating grain, fruit, vegetable and meat and dairy shortages for humans.

Loss of ecosystems
With only fungi around to recycle organic materials, all habitats – from deserts to rainforests, scrublands to pastures – would change for the worse.

Food chain collapse
Insect-eating animals would starve and die, which would mean less food – or none at all – for animals higher up the food chain.

Soil
If natural waste were not being composted, the soil would be starved of nutrients.

Uncontrolled spread
Uncontrolled spread of animals and plants that are eaten by insects.

The **dung beetle** lays **her eggs** inside small **sausages** of **dung**.

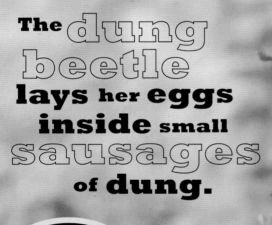

A dung beetle letting its feet cool by resting atop its dung ball

Fresh is best

Within 15 minutes of being excreted, a fresh pile of elephant dung can contain 4,000 dung beetles, all hard at work.

Follow the stars

Scientists have discovered that dung beetles navigate by the stars. When they put tiny hats on the beetles so they could not see upwards, the beetles became totally lost.

Did you know?

A dung beetle prefers plant-eater animal dung as it is more nutritious than meat-eater dung. But being less smelly than meat-eater dung, it takes longer for the beetle to find it.

A burying beetle will travel two kilometres to find a dead animal

Factfile

Mouthparts

There are five parts to an insect's mouth: upper lip, jaws, pincers, lower lip and a tongue-like organ. Each are modified to suit what the insect eats.

Housefly

The housefly drips saliva over its food to dissolve it. This is then soaked up by its sponge-like lips. A fly's mouth has no biting parts.

Butterfly

A butterfly sucks nectar through a tube which consists of two parts that 'zip' together. When not in use, the tube is coiled.

Ant

An ants uses its jaws to tear, puncture and grind its food and for defence. It also uses them for hunting and to move objects.

Pollination

Flies, butterflies, moths, wasps, bees, beetles, ants, midges and mosquitoes all collect nectar from flowers and in doing so spread pollen. Pollination helps plants produce seeds and fruits to ensure the next generation. Bees are the most efficient of all pollinators – a single colony can pollinate three million flowers a day.

Recycling

The burying beetle and its mate locate a dead body by the smell of its rotting flesh. The pair of beetles claim the corpse as their own and defend it from competitors. They dig around and under the corpse until it is buried, then the female lays her eggs in it. The young then feed on the carcass.

Control numbers

Aphids are insects that breed rapidly and destroy plants. A female will produce up to 100 female offspring that will reproduce within a week. Ladybirds are crucial in controlling aphid populations. They can eat over 5,000 aphids and other soft-bodied insects during their 12-month lifespan.

A seven-spotted ladybird about to eat an aphid

Helpful insects

Insects do vital work that **enriches** our lives in many ways. Bee **venom** has been used to treat arthritis and blowfly maggots can speed the **healing** of wounds. The tiny fruit fly opened the door to our understanding of **genetics**, and insects are used to assess the health of aquatic environments. Insects are a **nutritious** part of the diet of **African**, South American and Asian societies and they provide us with honey, beeswax, dyes and **tannin**, silk and more. **Domestic** animals like cows need insects to pollinate the plants they eat, so without them our **diet** would be very different.

Facts and figures

Social bees
There are 20,000 species and three types of social bees.

Bumble bees
Bumble bees are large and fluffy and they nest in shallow holes or in thick grass. These bees don't communicate, so learn by trial and error.

Honey bees
Honey bees nest in trees, and make wax combs in which honey can be produced and broods raised. Honey bees use signals to communicate.

Stingless bees
These bees have a stinger but rarely use it. They nest in trees or between rocks, storing their honey in beeswax (as used to make candles). Some communicate by sound vibrations.

Pollen baskets

A bee colony can gather 45 kg of pollen a year. It collects in 'baskets' on a bee's hind legs. Excess pollen is deposited on the next flower.

Bee vision

A bee's eyes are receptive to ultraviolet (UV), blue and green. It can't tell the difference between red and green, so may visit red flowers less. The UV patterns it sees guide it to the nectar.

A honey bee sucking nectar and gathering pollen in baskets on its rear legs

Did you know?

Manuka and jelly honey have antibacterial and anti-inflammatory properties that reduce infection and aid healing. The ancient Egyptians and Greeks knew all about this!

A silkworm feeding on mulberry leaves

Cocoons of silk

The silkworm, which is the caterpillar of the silkmoth, produces a strong, extremely fine thread that it uses to make its cocoon. One cocoon can produce a strand of silk 1.6 km long. To make half a kilogram of silk fabric requires 2,000-3,000 cocoons.

Bees dance

Honeybees perform a waggle dance to let other bees in the hive know the direction of nectar-rich flowers. If the nectar is near, the bee dances for a short period in circles; if far away, it dances for a longer period in a figure-of-eight. The direction of the figure-of-eight describes the location of the nectar in relation to the sun and the hive.

A **bee** will do **hundreds** of **trips** between **hive** and **flowers** every day.

A honeybee doing the waggle dance surrounded by bees

Food for thought

Insects could be the sustainable food of the future for Earth's growing population.

Pest control

Some 6,000 insects species are used by us as biological controls to limit the growth of certain plants and some insect populations.

Cochineal bugs

These tiny insects live on cacti paddles and cocoon themselves in waxy white material to protect them from the sun. When the females are crushed they produce a red dye that has been used since the 15th century. Called carmine, this dye is used in food products, from yoghurt to sausages, and in lipsticks.

A cluster of cochineal bugs in their protective 'cocoons'

Defence

Insects have many **enemies** – birds, lizards, spiders and other insects – and they have become masters of **survival**. Some keep out of the way and hide in dark corners or only come out at **night**, while others **display** colourful 'don't eat me, I taste nasty' patterns in broad daylight. **Camouflage** insects blend into their surroundings, while **copycat** (mimic) insects look like more **dangerous** insects. Some insects escape capture by their speed, while others **defend** themselves by attacking their predators with stingers, claws, spines and **toxic** secretions.

Facts and figures

Insects on the defence

Bombardier beetle
This small beetle ejects a toxic hot anal liquid spray over a predator.

Hoverfly
This insect mimics the appearance of a bee, but there is no sting in its tail!

Potato beetle
The larva of this insect covers itself in its own poisonous poo to put off any predators.

Carpenter ant
This Malaysian ant contracts its abdomen to explode poison-containing glands over the predator.

Saddleback caterpillar
When touched, the hairs on its body release an irritant.

Stick insect
This insect is camouflaged to look like a branch, but it also sways like a branch moving in the wind.

Did you know?

To make itself look larger and more dangerous, the five-centimetre-long spiny flower mantis raises its forewings that feature a pair of large yellow spiral eyespots.

Looking exactly like a flower, the orchid mantis waits for unsuspecting prey to come along

Clever glasswings

Glasswing butterflies almost disappear into any background with their transparent wings. Being hard to see gives these butterflies great protection from predators.

Bird droppings

To avoid becoming a meal for birds, some caterpillars look like bird droppings and they contort their bodies to mimic poo shapes!

A viceroy butterfly

A monarch butterfly

Clever mimics

When one insect assumes the appearance of another insect, it is called mimicry. The harmless copycat insect benefits from the feared reputation of its model. But viceroy and monarch butterflies both benefit from the mimicry. Each butterfly is unpalatable to different animals, but as they look the same, predators avoid both the viceroy and the monarch butterflies.

Warn then attack

When threatened the puss moth caterpillar raises its head, showing off its startling face, and its colourful filaments. If the predator persists, the caterpillar showers the predator with formic acid.

A puss moth caterpillar sends out a warning

Play dead

Ladybirds play dead, called thanatosis, when threatened. They fall to the ground where they are harder to find and stay very still.

Nasty smell

To deter predators the stink bug produces a nasty smell that wafts from holes in its abdomen.

Thorny issue

Thorn bugs spend most of their lives clinging to young branches, sucking their sap and laying their eggs in the branches. Their body is crowned with a hard, sharp horn that resembles a rose thorn. If a predator sees through the camouflage, it still has to get through the thorn bug's armour plating.

The thorn bug looks and stings like a rose thorn

Lobes on the **orchid mantis's** legs **resemble pink** and **white flower** petals.

Dangerous insects

We are all familiar with insects that deliver a nasty **sting** or painful bite and deposit foul things on our **food** that can make us very ill, but some insects are **deadly**. Even though only 30 of the 3,000 insects we frequently encounter are actually **harmful** to us they have made their mark on **human** history. Millions of people have died as a result of **diseases** spread by mosquitoes, thousands have been **attacked** by aggressive wasps and bees, and huge amounts of suffering has been caused when **swarming** insects, like **locusts**, have eaten and destroyed farmers' crops.

Facts and figures

Anopheles mosquitoes
The females transmit malaria. In 2013 there were 198 million cases of malaria in humans.

Rat fleas
Infected rat fleas can spread bubonic plague (Black Death). The last outbreak was in 1994.

Tsetse flies
These insects transmit sleeping sickness to humans. Some 70 million people in Africa are at risk.

Flies
These germ carriers spread diseases like typhoid fever.

Giant Asian hornets
These hornets inflict life-threatening stings.

Africanised 'killer' bees
These attack humans and animals and have caused deaths. The attack may be in response to being disturbed by noises or vehicle vibrations.

Destroy wood

Termites, carpenter ants and deathwatch beetles tunnel through wood. They destroy man-made structures from the inside.

Ancient cockroaches

Cockroach fossils that pre-date dinosaurs by 80 million years have been found. Cockroaches can go without food for a month and hold their breath for 40 minutes.

A cockroach is a helpful recycler of waste, but some spread disease

Did you know?

The world's heaviest insect, the giant burrowing cockroach, can be kept as a pet as it is not a disease-carrier. It grows to eight centimetres and digs metre-deep burrows.

Army ants mass around a bee

Massed ants

A colony of army ants will eat almost everything in their way because they have huge energy needs. They work together to attack other insects, small lizards and snakes and even chickens. To find enough food the colony is always on the move, so rarely makes a nest. Army ants have been known to troop through houses!

Locust swarms

A swarm of locusts can strip a field of crops in one hour. This can result in famine for human populations, especially for African farming communities. A swarm can cover 1,200 square km and there can be 40–80 million locusts in one square kilometre.

Chemical messages cause the desert locust to swarm

Cockroaches hide by day – they dislike the light – and come out when it's dark.

Evil weevils

The wheat weevil lays its eggs in stored grains. The larvae hatch and feed on the grain. They are sometimes found in bags of flour.

Black Death

Over a five year period in Europe in the 14th century the Black Death plague killed 25 million.

Deadliest insect

Some mosquito species transmit deadly diseases, including malaria and dengue and yellow fevers, that affect 700 million people a year and kill one million. They also transmit diseases to dogs and horses. When a mosquito bites – usually more than once – it injects disease-containing saliva.

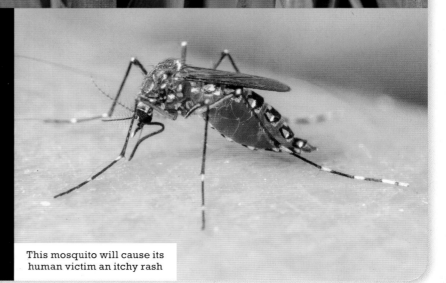
This mosquito will cause its human victim an itchy rash

Introducing spiders

There are **43,000–45,000** species of spiders with many more yet to be discovered. Only one **continent** – Antarctica – has escaped habitation by **arachnids**. Spiders have a hard external **skeleton** (exoskeleton) consisting of a fused head/thorax and an abdomen, **eight** legs, no antennae and all have the ability to bite with venom-injecting **fangs**. All spiders can produce silk, but not all spiders spin webs, and all except one species are **predatory** meat-eaters. Love them or hate them – **arachnophobia** (fear of spiders) affects one in six **people** – spiders are intriguing.

Facts and figures

Main groups
There are two main spider groups: web-spinners (their jaws open and close like a pair of pliers) and tarantulas (their jaws move up and down parallel to each other).

Hairy bodies
All spiders are covered with hairs. Some hairs help untangle silk, and others help them grip smooth surfaces. The hairs on a tarantula contain a mild venom.

Poor eyesight
Spiders have 6 or 8 eyes that only detect light and dark and basic shapes. Sensing vibrations makes up for their poor eyesight.

Pedipalps
These appendages near their mouth are used to manipulate their prey.

Clawed feet
Legs end in pairs of toothed claws, but web-spinners have an extra claw to hold web silk.

Did you know?

Each of a spider's eight legs has seven joints that gives them great flexibility for web spinning. To make a leg move, the spider fills or empties that leg's muscles with fluid.

A huntsman spider hunts at night for insects, small lizard and other spiders

Grow new limbs

A spider can replace lost legs when it moults. The new leg will look different from the original; it will takes a few months for it to grow to the right length and bulk.

Solitary spiders

Most spiders are solitary and aggressive to spiders of the same species, but some species live in colonies of 50,000 spiders.

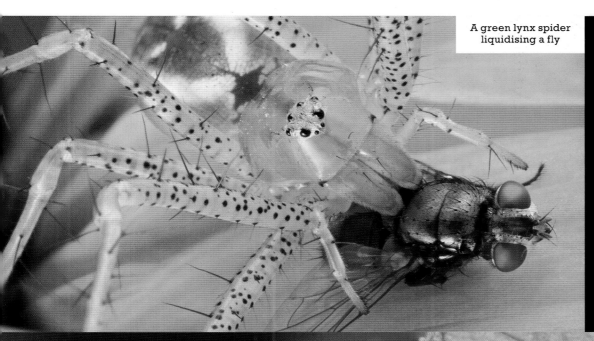

A green lynx spider liquidising a fly

How spiders eat

Spiders cannot ingest solid food. Instead, they vomit digestive juices on their kill and then grind it into a liquid that is sucked into the mouth. Some spiders vomit directly into the body of their prey, liquidising the organs and muscles that are then sucked out. This process is called external digestion.

Courtship mating

Tarantulas have a brief courtship in which the male extends his front legs towards the female. If she attacks, the male moves on. Other spiders may live in silk tents on the female's web until she is ready to mate. Some males offer a nuptial gift of food to the female to distract her during mating.

A male nursery web spider with a gift for the female

Feels vibrations

If anything moves within a few metres, a spider will pick up the vibrations and identify its source.

So many eyes

It is thought that each pair of eyes on a spider does a different job. Even so, their 6–8 eyes are not as effective as two human eyes.

Only 30 spider species are dangerous to humans.

Egg to spiderling

Some female spiders are attentive carers that will guard their egg sac, which contains up to 1,000 eggs, by carrying it around or by protecting its hiding place. Others abandon the egg sac. The eggs hatch and the spiderlings walk or 'balloon' away on silk threads. Most spiderlings will moult five times.

A female wolf spider with spiderlings on her abdomen

Web spinners

Half of all spiders use silk **threads** as a way to catch prey, but not all **web-spinners** spin webs. Some use the silk to line their 'home' inside a burrow or to tie up and **immobilise** prey; others use their silk to make **tempting** lures, trapping nets and abseil ropes. **Aquatic** insects build a silken raft as an underwater air pocket. Webs are designed to catch certain **prey** in specific locations, but a successful web has to **invisibly** cross the path of an insect, entangle the prey in the web and be **strong** enough not to break as the prey struggles to **escape** its inevitable end.

Facts and figures

All about spider silk

Creating silk
It is formed in the spider's silk glands and is made of proteins. Spiders can have up to five types of glands to produce varieties of 'dry' or sticky silk.

Dry or sticky?
Silk is 'dry' when spun. Depending on the purpose of the silk, the spider can then coat it with sticky silk that will trap prey.

Very strong
Spider silk is the strongest known natural fibre. It is used by some Indo-Pacific fishermen to make fishing nets.

Spinning
Spinnerets on the rear of the abdomen spin the liquid silk as it flows out of tubes. The silk then hardens in air.

Undissolvable
Spider silk cannot be dissolved in water.

Spiders are born knowing how to spin their own type of web.

The super-strong web of the golden silk orb-weaving spider

Did you know?

The banded garden spider's web is almost invisible except for a zigzag pattern, which could make the web visible to larger animals that would otherwise damage the web.

Orb weavers

Orb weaver spiders can produce webs six metres high and two metres wide. The spiders litter the web with insect husks to deter birds flying into the web and destroying it.

Abseil to safety

Spiders can use a length of silk, called a dragline, to abseil away from danger. They can climb the thread back to their web when safe.

An orb-weaver may spin 100 webs in its 12-month lifespan

Spiral web

Orb-weavers build the familiar sticky, flat spiral web. After floating a thread on the wind to a fixing point, the spider drops 4–5 vertical threads to create a silk scaffold. Multiple threads run out from the centre, and then the spiral is created. The web is made or repaired each evening.

Trapping net

Dangling from a thread a net-casting spider spins a sticky blue-white net that it holds with its front four legs. When an insect passes below, the spider abseils down and traps the insect under the net. The spider wraps its prey in silk to immobilise it, paralyses it with venom and then eats it.

A long-legged net-casting spider readies its net

Bolas spider

Named after a throwing weapon, bolas spiders hang from a dragline, a moth-attracting silk ball suspended below it. When a moth approaches, the spider spins the ball like a lasso entangling the moth. When caught in a normal web, the moth's wing scales shed on the sticky silk and the moth escapes.

A bolas spider spins its sticky lure lasso-style

Factfile

Other spider specialists

Spiders have developed so many survival methods scientists believe that its complex brain occupies 80 per cent of its body.

Wraparound spider
This spider conceals itself by day by wrapping its curved abdomen around a branch and staying still.

Spitting spider
This spider spits a poison over its prey in a 'Z' pattern, immobilising it in 1/700th of a second.

Goldenrod crab spider
This spider changes colour to camouflage itself. It can turn yellow in 30 days and white in seven days.

Long-horned orb weaver
This small spider has two long horns sprouting from its abdomen. The horns may make it appear larger.

Jumpers and swimmers

Jumping spiders are known for their ability to **leap** great distances for their small size and for their excellent **vision**. Four of their eight **eyes** look forwards and four upwards, and all can look up, down, left and right. They can see **prey** that is 30–40 cm away, and when it is within reach they pump fluid into their rear legs and **pounce**. Water and **fishing** spiders live all or part of their lives on or under the water. They do not have **gills** to breathe underwater, so they have adapted to take air with them when they **dive**. The diving bell spider is so at home in water it can remain **submerged** for a day.

Facts and figures

Jumping spiders
Species: Around 5,000 species.
Size: 1 cm in length.
Use of silk: They use silk as draglines and to mark their 'home' and protect their eggs.
Venom: These spiders avoid any contact with humans and their venom is not dangerous.

Water spiders
Species: Only one species – the diving bell – lives permanently in water.
Size: 1.5 cm in length.
Use of silk: The 'diving bell', which is used when eating, moulting and mating, is made of silk.
Venom: The diving bell spider's venom can cause swelling and fever.

Did you know?

The jumping spider can leap up to 50 times its body length. It will stalk prey, like this hoverfly, before pumping fluid into its leg muscles, securing a dragline and jumping.

A colourful male jumping spider eating a fly

Home up high

One jumping spider has made Mount Everest in the Himalayas home, making it Earth's highest resident. The Latin name of this spider means 'standing above everything'.

Food blown in

The Mount Everest jumping spider feeds on flies and springtails carried by the wind that sweeps up the peak.

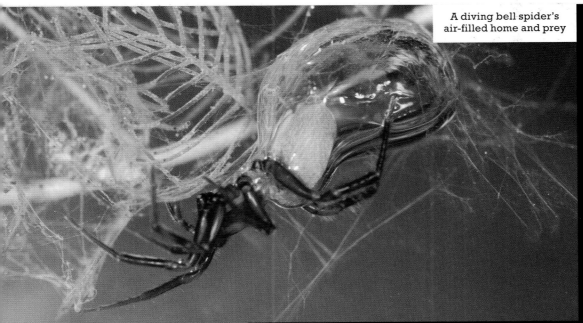
A diving bell spider's air-filled home and prey

Water spiders

The diving bell spider breathes air in the normal way, which is why it must transport bubbles of air to its submerged 'diving bell' home in streams and ponds. This spider feeds on mosquito larvae and planktonic crustaceans and can stay submerged in its diving bell for up to a day.

Fishing spider

These spiders usually live near water and catch aquatic insects and fish by running on the water or by diving into it. They detect prey by sensing its vibrations. They snare the catch in their claw-tipped front legs and inject it with venom. When diving, they are enclosed in an envelope of air.

A fishing spider has caught a fish dinner

Walking on water

Fishing spiders walk on water by spreading their light weight between their long legs. The hairs on their body and legs repel water.

Diving bell tunnel

During courtship the male diving bell spider links his home to the female's with a silk tunnel.

Jumping spiders use lateral eyes to sense motion and principle eyes to judge distance.

Amazing displays

Australian peacock spiders, related to jumping spiders, put on fantastic courtship displays. In the presence of the female, the male waves or claps its rear legs in the air and opens flaps that reveal colourful patterns on its abdomen. As the female approaches, the male dances from side to side.

A peacock spider shaking its decorated abdomen

Hunters and trappers

These spiders catch their prey by **hunting** them down or by setting **traps**. Though they can produce silk, they do not make spiral webs. Hunting spiders like **tarantulas**, which includes the Goliath **bird-eating** spider, and wolf spiders rush at their prey and inject venom. **Ambush** spiders wait for their prey to come to them. **Trapdoor** spiders dig a hole topped with a 'door' and when prey steps over the **tripwires** that run from the trap, the spider rushes from its hole and attacks. **Pursewebs** and **funnel-webs** ambush their prey from inside a silken tube.

Tarantulas hunt at night using touch rather than sight.

An orange baboon tarantula shows her fangs when defending her nest

Did you know?

There is only one vegetarian spider. It lives in Central America and feeds on wattle plants. It is called *Bagheera kiplingi* and was named after the panther in *The Jungle Book*.

Hair as a weapon

When threatened, tarantulas tear hairs from their abdomen and throw them at the attacker. The hairs contain an irritant that gives the tarantula time to escape or attack.

Freeze or rear?

When alarmed, trapdoor spiders will freeze on the spot, but funnel-web spiders will rear up and display their fangs.

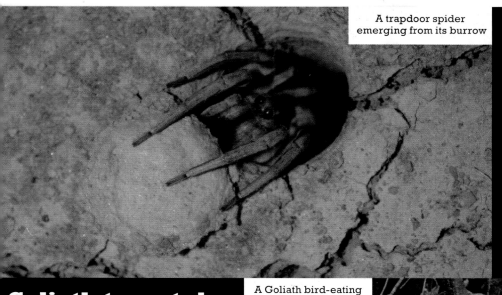
A trapdoor spider emerging from its burrow

Trapdoor spiders

There are numerous species of trapdoor spiders and while all dig a hole, some cover the hole with leaves and dirt rather than a door. The hole is where the female lays her eggs, and she will defend her brood strongly. Spiderlings will remain in the hole for a few months before digging their own burrow.

Factfile

Other hunters and trappers

Some spiders use their highly developed senses not only to catch prey but also to protect themselves and their offspring.

Mouse spider
The mouse spider digs a 20–50-cm-long 'mouse-like' burrow with two trapdoors and a chamber to keep its offspring safe.

Goliath tarantula

The Goliath bird-eating spider measures up to 30 cm across and can weigh 170 grams. It is a predatory hunter that eats mainly toads and earthworms, but will eat rodents, lizards, snakes and even birds. Its venom is regarded as harmless to humans.

Ambush webs

Purseweb and funnel-web spiders lie in wait in their ground-built sock- and funnel-shaped webs. When prey lands on the purseweb's nest, the spider stabs its fangs through the silk and pulls the insect inside. The funnel-web rushes out to envenomate its victim. These spiders, bar the Sydney funnel-web, are not dangerous to humans.

A Goliath bird-eating spider

Wolf spider
A wolf spider carrying her egg sac. Parasitoid wasps can lay their eggs in the egg sac without the female spider realising it.

Green bluebottle
This tarantula with its blue legs, shiny green body and orange abdomen is one of the world's most colourful spiders.

The killing fangs of the Atlantic purseweb spider

Deadly spiders

Of all the tens of **thousands** of spider species, only about a dozen are regarded as highly **dangerous** to humans and even fewer have caused deaths. Though all spiders have **venom**, most of it is too weak to affect humans. Spider **fangs**, which are designed to deliver venom to a small **animal**, are usually inadequate to break our skin and to deliver sufficient venom. **Antivenoms**, which were first produced in the late **1880s**, have reduced fatalities from spider **bites** enormously, but if you spot any of the spiders on these pages in real life, it is always best to keep your **distance**!

Facts and figures

Most dangerous spiders

Sydney funnel-web
Its venom can cause death in 15 minutes. There have been no deaths since 1981 when the antivenom was made available.

Black and red widow spiders
These cause severe pain, vomiting and difficulty breathing. It can be fatal to the elderly and children. Antivenom available.

Red-back spider
The venom causes pain, sweating and increased heart rate. No deaths since 1956. An antivenom is available.

Yellow sac spider
Its venom can destroy and damage cells causing severe wounds.

Brazilian wandering spider
The toxic venom affects the nervous system and can cause death. An antivenom is available.

Nest flooded

The Sydney funnel-web is found in an area 160 km around Sydney, Australia. This aggressive spider is sometimes found in swimming pools or homes after heavy rain has flooded its nest.

Funnel web colony

Although normally solitary, colonies of up to 100 female Sydney funnel-web spiders have been discovered.

The Sydney funnel-web spider with venom dripping from its downward pointing fangs

Did you know?

The false widow is often confused with the black widow, but its skull-shaped markings are cream. The false widow's venomous bite is no more severe than a bee sting.

A female red-back spider making its web

The red-back

The red-back spider can be identified by a red stripe on the top of its abdomen and an hourglass-shaped mark underneath. Its large web catches flies, grasshoppers and beetles that it envenomates with its strongs fangs. The red-back spider is a cousin of the black widow.

The wanderer

Aggressive and venomous, the Brazilian wandering spider grows to 12 cm and can move very quickly. During the day it hides in dark places, including houses and cars, and hunts at night. When disturbed it raises its front legs, its red jaws become visible and it sways from side to side.

A Brazilian wandering spider devours a moth

A **Sydney funnel web's** fangs are **larger** than those of a **brown snake.**

Table manners

Some spiders chew their prey before vomiting digestive fluid onto it and drinking the liquid remains.

Spider symptoms

Bites from a black widow can cause fevers, nausea, vomiting, headaches, rashes, abdominal pain and muscle cramping.

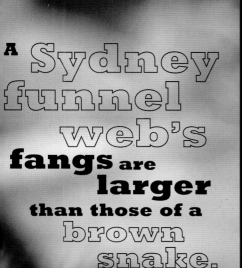

Yellow sac spider

Measuring 0.5 cm this pale spider is easily overlooked. It has extra long front legs, which it waves about when chasing prey, and it will head indoors in cold weather. During the day it retreats to a silk tube. It is not deadly, but it's thought to be responsible for more hospital-reported bites than any other spider.

The straw-coloured yellow sac spider

Glossary

Abdomen
Body segment that contains the digestive, reproductive and breathing organs.

Adaptation
Having functions to survive in a habitat.

Antenna
Moveable pair of sensing organs on the head.

Antivenom (antivenin)
An antibody serum against a venom.

Arachnids
Spiders and scorpions.

Biological control
Controlling a pest with a natural predator.

Camouflage
Disguise that blends into the habitat.

Caterpillar
The larva stage of a butterfly or moth.

Chrysalis
The pupa of a butterfly.

Cocoon
Silk covering that surrounds a pupa.

Colony
A group of the same species living together.

Courtship
The time before a male and female mate.

Dragline
A silk thread used by spiders as a safety line when jumping or leaving their nest.

Ecosystem
A community of living things that are connected together in a habitat.

Envenomate
When a spider or insect bites or stings its prey and injects venom.

Exoskeleton
The hard outer shell that is an external skeleton.

Fangs
The pair of pointed 'teeth' used by spiders to pierce the body of their prey and to inject venom.

Habitat
A living creature's natural place to live.

Host
A living creature that is home and food source to another living thing.

Incubator
A place where eggs can hatch safely.

Insect
An animal with an exoskeleton, three body segments and six legs.

Larva (larvae, plural)
The worm-like stage of an immature insect.

Life cycle
The stages of a living thing from birth to death.

Mating
Another name for reproducing or breeding offspring.

Metamorphosis
The process of changing from an egg to larva or nymph, sometimes followed by pupa, to mature mating adult.

Moult
The process of shedding the exoskeleton.

Nectar
Sugary liquid found in plants, especially flowers.

Nuptial gift
Food given by the male to the female before mating.

Nymph
A life cycle stage of some insects.

Parasitoid or parasitic
An insect that lays its eggs inside or on a host.

Pedipalps
Two pincers used by spiders to hold things.

Pollinating
Carrying pollen from one plant and depositing it on another plant in order to fertilise it.

Predator
An animal that preys on other animals for food.

Prey
An animal that is natural food for another animal.

Proboscis
The tube-like mouthpart used to suck liquid.

Pupa (pupae, plural)
In metamorphosis this is when the adult is formed inside a cocoon.

Social
An animal that lives with similar animals in a colony or community. Non-social animals usually live alone.

Spider
An animal with an exoskeleton, two body segments and eight legs.

Spiderling
An immature spider.

Spinneret
The silk-producing organ in the abdomen of a spider and some insects.

Spiracles
Small openings on the abdomen through which an insect (and some spider species) breathes.

Swarm
A huge group of insects.

Thorax
The middle segment of the body where legs and wings are found.

Toxic
A substance that is poisonous or harmful.

Venom
Poisonous substance that is usually injected into prey by a predator.

Index